KIDS IN HISTORY

How Did Kids Live in Ancient Greece?

BY MEGAN QUICK

Gareth Stevens PUBLISHING

Please visit our website, www.garethstevens.com. For a free color catalog of all our high-quality books, call toll free 1-800-542-2595 or fax 1-877-542-2596.

Library of Congress Cataloging-in-Publication Data
Names: Quick, Megan, author.
Title: How did kids live in ancient Greece? / Megan Quick.
Description: Buffalo, New York : Gareth Stevens Publishing, 2024. | Series: Kids in history | Includes bibliographical references and index. | Audience: Grades 2-3
Identifiers: LCCN 2023009664 (print) | LCCN 2023009665 (ebook) | ISBN 9781538288191 (library binding) | ISBN 9781538288184 (paperback) | ISBN 9781538288207 (ebook)
Subjects: LCSH: Children–Greece–History–To 1500–Juvenile literature. | Greece–Social conditions–To 146 B.C.–Juvenile literature. | Greece–Civilization–To 146 B.C.–Juvenile literature.
Classification: LCC DE61.C4 Q55 2024 (print) | LCC DE61.C4 (ebook) | DDC 938–dc23/eng/20230307
LC record available at https://lccn.loc.gov/2023009664
LC ebook record available at https://lccn.loc.gov/2023009665

Portions of this work were originally authored by Sarah Machajewski and published as *A Kid's Life in Ancient Greece*. All new material in this edition was authored by Megan Quick.

First Edition

Published in 2024 by
Gareth Stevens Publishing
2544 Clinton Street
Buffalo, NY 14224

Designer: Jen Schoembs
Editor: Megan Quick

Photo credits: Cover, pp. 1 (Greece), 5 Lambros Kazan/Shutterstock.com; cover, p. 1 (boy) Gelpi/Shutterstock.com; cover (background), p.1 (background), series art (background) Login/Shutterstock.com; p. 5 Tomas Marek /Shutterstock.com; p. 7 Simeon Netchev/World History Encyclopedia/worldhistory.org; p. 9 tan_tan/Shutterstock.com; p. 11 Jane Tregelles/ Alamy.com; p. 13 ilbusca/iStock.com; p. 15 Morphart Creation/Shuterstock.com; p. 17 clu/iStock.com; p. 19 North Wind Picture Archives/Alamy.com; p. 21 INTERFOTO/Alamy.com.

Printed in the United States of America

CPSIA compliance information: Batch #CS24GS: For further information contact Gareth Stevens at 1-800-542-2595.

Find us on

Contents

Leaving Their Mark 4
A Divided Land 6
Basic Rights 8
At Home in Greece 10
Greek Fashion 12
Time to Eat 14
School Days 16
Fun and Games 18
Myths Live On 20
Glossary 22
For More Information 23
Index 24

Words in the glossary appear in **bold** type the first time they are used in the text.

Leaving Their Mark

The ancient Greek **civilization** lasted from about 1200 BCE to 323 BCE. Its people set up governments and cities. They created art, writings, and sports. They loved learning and coming up with new ideas. Ancient Greece existed long ago, but it shaped the world we live in today.

Would you like to have lived in ancient Greece? Many things were different for kids back then: food, homes, clothes, and games. Read on to find out more about this **unique** time and place.

Life in the Past

The ancient Greeks didn't call themselves "Greeks." They were "Hellenes" or "Έλληνες" in the Greek language.

Athens is the capital of modern Greece. The city contains many remains from ancient times, such as the temple called the Parthenon, seen here.

A Divided Land

Today, Greece is a single country. But in ancient times, it was made up of many city-states. A city-state was a city and all the land around it. Each had its own government, laws, and military.

Two important city-states were Athens and Sparta. People in both places spoke the same language and prayed to the same gods. But they had many differences. In Athens, people were interested in education, art, and **philosophy.** Sparta was a **warlike** state. Life there centered on training for battle and fighting wars.

Life in the Past

In ancient Greece, people **worshipped** many gods. They believed the gods controlled everything about the world, such as weather or crops. The Greeks made offerings at temples to keep the gods happy.

Ancient Greece included more land than modern Greece does.

Basic Rights

The ancient Greeks didn't all have the same rights. Only men were citizens. This meant only men could vote and decide how to run the city-state. In most of Greece, including Athens, women couldn't own land. Their main role was to take care of the family.

Women in Sparta had more rights and freedom. While boys trained to be soldiers, girls exercised so they could become strong. Women could own land. They made more decisions at home since the men were often away at war.

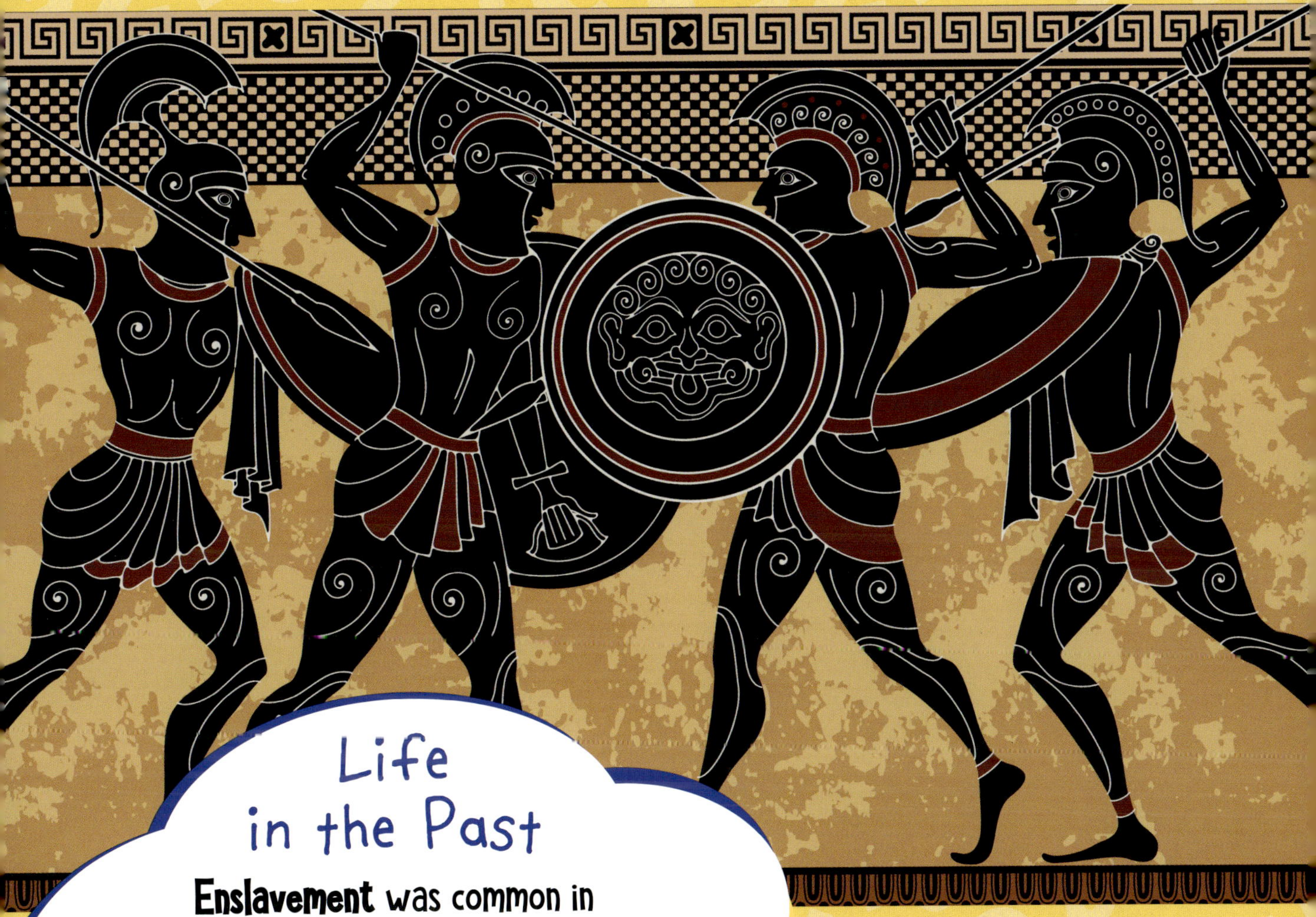

Life in the Past

Enslavement was common in ancient Greece. In Athens, households included about three or four enslaved people. They were forced to work for no money. Many enslaved people were children.

This picture shows warriors, or soldiers, from Sparta in battle.

At Home in Greece

Children in ancient Greece spent much of their time at home. Most houses were small and plain, even for wealthy people. They were made of wood or mud brick, with a stone floor. The windows were small and had shutters, a kind of cover to keep out the sun.

Most homes were built around a courtyard, which is a small, outdoor space in the center of the house. Poor families would cook outside over a fire. Everyone would sleep in one room.

Life in the Past

Most families in ancient Greece didn't have bathrooms in their homes. They used a bucket or walked to a nearby stream to get clean.

This Greek home on the island of Kos was built to look exactly like the houses of ancient Greece.

Greek Fashion

Greece can get quite hot, so clothing was loose and light. Many ancient Greeks made their own cloth. They wore **tunics** called chitons (KY-tuhnz). Chitons came together at the shoulders and were belted at the waist. Women wore floor-length chitons, while children and men wore chitons that ended at the knee.

Greeks wore a piece of cloth around their shoulders called a himation (hih-MAA-tee-ahn). Himations were thin in the summer and thicker in the winter. Many ancient Greeks wore sandals, but some went barefoot too.

Life in the Past

Young children in ancient Greece often didn't wear clothes at all, especially at home.

This picture shows family members in ancient Greece wearing different styles of chitons.

Time to Eat

Ancient Greeks grew their own food. They enjoyed fruit, such as olives, grapes, figs, and apples. They also grew wheat for bread and ate fish and eggs. But olives were the most important food in ancient Greece. The city-states were full of olive trees. Greeks crushed olives to make olive oil. They used the oil for cooking.

Ancient Greeks didn't use forks or knives. They ate with their fingers! Girls and women weren't allowed to have meals with the men. They ate in the kitchen.

Ancient Greeks often laid on couches while they ate.

Life in the Past

Ancient Greeks didn't use napkins when they ate. They wiped their hands on pieces of bread. Then they gave the bread to their dogs.

School Days

Boys and girls in ancient Greece received very different educations. In Athens, boys went to school starting at age 7. They learned reading, writing, music, and **poetry.** They ran and wrestled, a type of fighting, to stay fit. Girls didn't go to school. They learned to read and write at home. They also learned how to cook and make cloth.

In Sparta, boys learned how to become soldiers. They also learned how to read and write, but this was not as important as learning how to fight.

Life in the Past

At age 7, boys in Sparta had to leave home and attend military camps. They slept on hard beds and didn't have much food or clothing. The government wanted them to be tough.

This picture shows boys receiving different lessons from their teachers.

Fun and Games

When the children of ancient Greece weren't in school, they loved playtime. Young Spartans played games that showed their strength and fighting skills. Boys in Athens often wrestled for fun.

Like all children, ancient Greeks enjoyed toys. They had clay dolls and rattles. They played with tops and balls. Many believe the ancient Geeks invented the yo-yo! But by age 13, it was time to give up toys. Children of this age offered their toys to the gods. It was the sign of becoming an adult.

Life in the Past

The ancient Greeks invented another kind of game: the Olympics. The first Olympic games were held in 776 BCE in Olympia. They were held to honor the god Zeus.

Here, boys run a foot race in ancient Greece.

Myths Live On

Children in ancient Greece grew up hearing stories called **myths.** These stories were about the gods and goddesses. Many of them included magic and monsters. Myths taught young Greeks lessons about what is good and bad. You can still read the same Greek myths that children heard from their parents thousands of years ago.

Being a kid in ancient Greece was not easy for many. But we can thank the Greeks for the parts of their **culture** that live on today.

Life in the Past

There are many things you may use in your daily life that come from the ancient Greeks. These include alarm clocks, umbrellas, maps, showers, and cheesecake.

Gods and goddesses were at the center of Greek myths. The Greeks used these stories to explain all parts of life.

Glossary

civilization: Organized society with written records and laws.

culture: The beliefs and ways of life of a group of people.

enslavement: The state of being owned by another person and forced to work without pay.

myth: A story that was told by a people to explain a practice, belief, or natural event.

philosophy: A system of thought made to try to understand the nature of that which is real.

poetry: Writing in verse that sometimes tells a story.

tunic: A usually belted, knee-length garment worn by ancient Greeks and Romans.

unique: One of a kind.

warlike: Fit for, or fond of, war

worship: To honor as a god.

For More Information

Books

Hubbard, Ben. *How We Lived in Ancient Times.* London, England: Welbeck Children's, 2020.

O'Neill, Sean. *50 Things You Didn't Know About Ancient Greece.* South Egremont, MA: Red Chair Press, 2020.

Stokes, Jonathan W. *The Thrifty Guide to Ancient Greece: A Handbook for Time Travelers.* New York, NY: Puffin Books, 2019.

Websites

BBC – Bitesize Ancient Greeks
www.bbc.co.uk/bitesize/topics/z87tn39
Learn more about ancient Greeks through videos, activities, and quizzes.

DK Find Out! Ancient Greece
www.dkfindout.com/us/history/ancient-greece/
Click on the map to find out more about important people and places of ancient Greece.

Ducksters: Ancient Greece for Kids
www.ducksters.com/history/ancient_greece.php
Check out fun facts about the history and people of ancient Greece.

Publisher's note to educators and parents: Our editors have carefully reviewed these websites to ensure that they are suitable for students. Many websites change frequently, however, and we cannot guarantee that a site's future contents will continue to meet our high standards of quality and educational value. Be advised that students should be closely supervised whenever they access the internet.

Index

art, 4, 6
Athens, 6, 8, 9, 16, 18
cities, 4, 5, 6, 8
clothing, 4, 12, 13, 16, 17
education, 4, 6, 16, 17
enslavement, 9
family, 8, 10, 11
farming, 7, 14
food, 4, 10, 14, 15, 16, 17
government, 4, 6, 8, 17
homes, 4, 10, 11
Kos, 11
language, 5, 6
laws, 6, 8
literature, 16
military, 6, 8, 9, 16, 17
music, 16
myth, 20, 21
Olympics, 19
Parthenon, 5
philosophy, 6
play, 4, 18, 19
religion, 6, 7, 18, 19, 20, 21
Sparta, 6, 8, 16, 17, 18
sport, 4
temple, 5, 7
war, 6, 8, 9
women, 8, 12, 14